數字故事

THE NUMBER STORY

SMALL BOOK ONE

ENGLISH - TRADITIONAL CHINESE

Numbers Teach Children Their Number Names

written and illustrated by

MISS ANNA

Early Reader Edition of *The Number Story 1*
Bronze Medal Winner, 2016 Wishing Shelf Book Award

Copyright © 2018 by Jieeun Woo
Illustrations © Jieeun Woo

Cover by | Lumpy Publishing
Layout by | Lumpy Publishing
Translated by Carol Gwo
Coloring by Jieeun Woo and Maria

All rights reserved. No part of this book may be reproduced or transmitted in any form or by any means whatsoever, including photocopying, recording or by any information storage and retrieval system, without written permission from the publisher and/or author: missanna@missannabooks.com.

Library of Congress Control Number: 2018902040

Names: Miss Anna, author.
Title: Number story : numbers teach children their number names / Miss Anna.
Description: Portland, OR: Lumpy Publishing, 2018.
Identifiers: ISBN 978-1-945977-14-5 | LCCN 2018902040
Summary: The pictures and rhymes present stories which introduce numbers 0-10.
Subjects: LCSH Numeration--English--Pictorial works--Juvenile literature. | BISAC JUVENILE NONFICTION /
Languages: English—Traditional Chinese
Classification: LCC QA141.3 .M57 2018 | DDC 513—dc23

Publisher: Lumpy Publishing
Website: www.missannabooks.com
Email: missanna@missannabooks.com

Paperback: ISBN 978-1-945977-14-5
Printed in the U.S.A.   1 3 5 7 9 10 8 6 4 2

想學習數字名稱嗎？

It is very easy and a lot of fun!

這很容易且有趣！

Say-along our little jingle

跟我們唱兒歌。

starting from Number One!

我們從一開始!

1
ONE   looks like my one finger.
一 就像一根手指。

ONE!

2
TWO   trails a tail.
二   像一條小尾巴。

嗖 嗖~
SWISH!
SWISH!

THREE has bumps.

三 有不平的坑窪。

BUMPY! 顛簸！

4

FOUR carries a sail.

四 揚帆起航。

4
起航！
A SAIL!

5

FIVE   is a racing track.

五 像是一條跑道。

VROOM
哦也！
1

6

SIX   curves like a snail.

六 又曲又彎像蝸牛。

蝸牛！

A SNAIL!

7

SEVEN   has a sharp angle.

七 有尖銳的角。

OUCH!
哎哟!

8

EIGHT   is rollercoaster rails.

八 像是過山車軌道。

呦呼！
YIPPEE!

NINE   is a bubble on a stick.

九 泡泡在棍子的頂部。

A BUBBLE! 泡泡!

10

TEN is an eye of a whale.

十　鯨魚的一隻眼睛。

眨眼！
WINK!

And
和
0
ZERO is an empty pail.
零 像是一個空桶。

IT'S
EMPTY!
空的！

Thank you for playing with us today.

We had a lot of fun too!

感謝你今天和我們一起玩。

我們也有很多樂趣！

We are your Number friends,
Zero to Ten,
Who will be here for you~
我們是你的數字朋友，從零到十。
我們在這裡等待你的光臨。

Bye-bye now!
See you again soon!
再見！
期待很快再見到你！

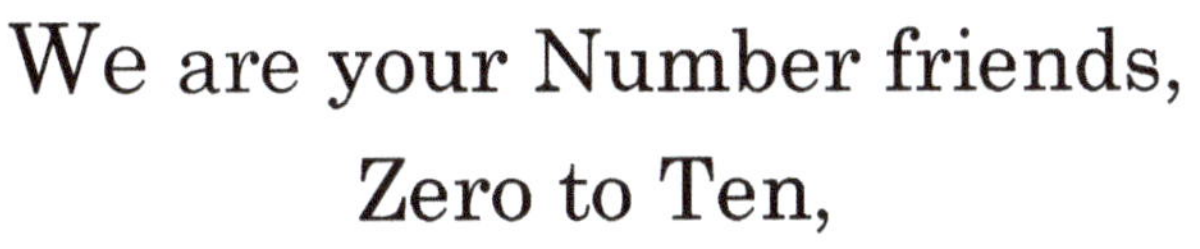

The Numbers are *SINGING* too!

To sing-a-long, look for Miss Anna Number Story
at your favorite music store like iTUNES.

MP3

Numbers 0-10 IDENTIFYING & COUNTING	Numbers 11-20 & Ordinals first, second, third...	Numbers 0-100 & Place Values ones, tens, hundreds...	About Clocks & Telling Time hours, minutes, seconds
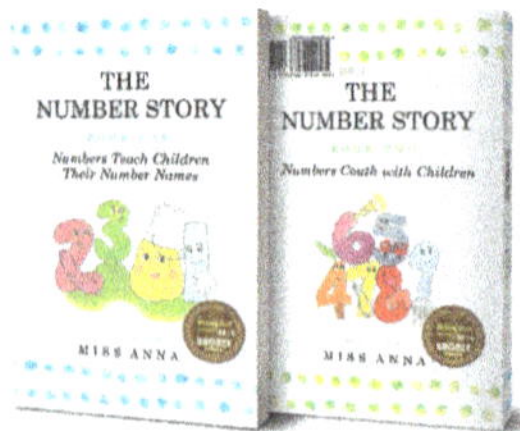			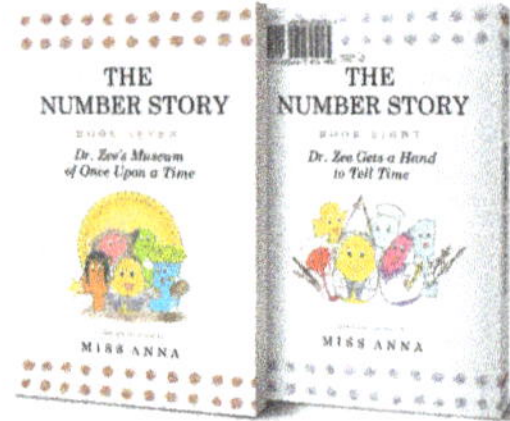
Number Story 1 & 2 isbn: 978-0-996216-48-7	Number Story 3 & 4 isbn: 978-1-945977-01-5	Number Story 5 & 6 isbn: 978-1-945977-06-0	Number Story 7 & 8 isbn: 978-1-949320-40-4

For more Miss Anna books to love,
visit us at

www.missannabooks.com

Numbers are working hard all over the world!
Come Travel the World with Us!

www.ingramcontent.com/pod-product-compliance
Lightning Source LLC
Chambersburg PA
CBHW040902070726
47599CB00035B/2276